IMAGES
of America

SALINE COUNTY

Assaria Lutheran Church, built in 1883 by Scottish and English settlers, was originally a framed church. The stone church was built in 1916 by the Swedes. The new church, pictured here in 1916, was built because the Swedes did not like wooden structures, as they often caught fire. Also, they needed a bigger church because of their expanding congregation. (Courtesy of the Salina Public Library, Campbell Room of Kansas Research, Dale Weiss Collection.)

ON THE COVER: Pictured on November 24, 1892, the Lincoln Locomotive crashed while on its way from Culver to Salina. Six of the grain cars were destroyed due to defective railings. It is still unknown what caused the rail to collapse. No people or livestock were killed in this horrific crash. Unidentified people stand around the wreckage. (Courtesy of the Salina Public Library, Campbell Room of Kansas Research, Dale Weiss Collection.)

IMAGES
of America

SALINE COUNTY

Faith Dincolo and Dustin Ray Shannon

ARCADIA
PUBLISHING

Published by Arcadia Publishing
Charleston, South Carolina

Library of Congress Control Number: 2013951877

For all general information, please contact Arcadia Publishing:
Telephone 843-853-2070
Fax 843-853-0044
E-mail sales@arcadiapublishing.com
For customer service and orders:
Toll-Free 1-888-313-2665

Visit us on the Internet at www.arcadiapublishing.com

*To the brave pioneers and immigrants who explored
and settled the Kansas territories, creating a rich
history and survivalist spirit that endures today.*

CONTENTS

ACKNOWLEDGMENTS

The authors would like to thank Jason Humphries, Lydia Rollins, and Jesse Darland at Arcadia Publishing; Tom Holmquist; Angela A. Allen, head of information services at the Salina Public Library in Salina, Kansas; Barbara Mulvihill at the Salina Public Library; Salina Public Library, Kansas Research Room and Dale Weiss Collection; Laura's Antiques in Salina, Kansas; Peggy Harrington; Nancy Sherbert; Kansas Historical Society; Leola K. Burch Hall and Janet Paradee; Terri Levin Wally Hitchcock; and Ty Little and John Lokke of City Arts.

Unless otherwise noted, images in this volume appear courtesy of the Salina Public Library. Images are drawn from the Campbell Room of Kansas Research (CRKR); the Campbell Room of Kansas Research, Dale Weiss Collection (DWC); and the Campbell Room of Kansas Research, Magnuson Collection (MC).

INTRODUCTION

Saline County towns and communities evolved around boom and bust years, seeing the fall of many towns, such as Chico, and the rise of other towns, including Smolan. The Town of Saline was the first established settlement in the county as of 1855. Early explorers Preston Plumb and Alfred Price, amongst others, followed the Fort Riley Military Wagon Road. They discovered an empty cabin that was built by Coote Lombard, an early engineer working for the Kansas territorial government. The structure was right next to a plank bridge that crossed the Saline River. This cabin led way to the second-earliest town, Mariposa, which was established 1856. Due to difficult border ruffians and angry Native Americans, they only lasted a few months in the cabin.

Gotthart Schippel was the earliest permanent settler of the land outside of East Salina, settling in the now-empty Mariposa cabin. He was the largest landholder in the state of Kansas. There was a saying that you could not walk from Salina to New Cambria without stepping on his land. Under a proclamation issued by Rev. Eric Forsse, the Swedish people flocked to the towns of Bavaria, Smolan, and others. It was said at one time that hundreds of Swedes a month were coming by train, with most living in dire poverty as they learned to work the land.

Camp Phillips was a town that came and went in a three-year time period during World War II. The city was erected and completely dismantled during those few years, leaving only a few traces of its existence on the land. Chico almost completely disappeared, leaving only the scars of railroad tracks. Other extinct towns are hidden in Saline County, leaving behind old schoolhouses and churches or remains of houses.

The railroad played a huge role in the boom or bust of towns. Native Americans lost their lands and lifestyles as the train made its way across Saline County. Brookville and Salina both were embattled in deadly confrontations as the railroad continued to lay tracks and open up the land to eastern settlers.

Brookville was platted as a railroad town in 1867, but a few years after it was established, the railroad shut down there and moved to Salina. Brookville had other means of surviving, including an active cattle and farming community. The Brookville Hotel played an active role in the town and through the years has evolved, decayed, and eventually relocated to Abilene. Brookville also has a frontier-town flavor. In 1874, a fight between saloon owner Harry Bonham and two brothers resulted in the death of both the brothers. Bonham was put in jail and nearly lynched, but Brookville townspeople rallied together to save him from being hung, and he was sentenced to life in prison.

Bridgeport grew at the end of the Civil War in 1865 under the Homestead Act and manifest destiny. It was originally populated by Swedish immigrants. The Bridgeport Mill produced highly prized flours, including the Belle of Bridgeport flour. Bridgeport, named after a bridge that crossed over the Smokey Hill River, was known as the cheese capital of Kansas.

Falun grew under the influence of Maj. Eric Forsee, a Swedish immigrant who served in the Civil War. He brought a group of Swedish settlers from Illinois to Saline County and settled the Falun area. In 1886, the railroad came through and helped grow Falun into a town with a post office, blacksmith, and bank. Camp Phillips was located in the area, and along with hard weather and difficult economic times, Falun struggled but has survived.

New Cambria was settled around 1873, and the railroad passed right by the little town until Simon Donmeyer built a depot for it to stop at. He proved successful as the train made regular stops to his depot.

Gypsum was also developed because of the railroad. In 1887, John Klingman and Jonathan Tinkler developed a town with a roller mill. The town is most famous for its gypsum deposits, which were mined and used to make plaster. Gypsum also was known for its cheese factory.

Assaria also had a flour roller mill. Many Scottish and English people settled in Assaria but moved on because of the difficult weather. The Swedes soon took over the area, building a Lutheran church and schools. Like the other small towns of Saline County, Assaria struggled with the Great Depression and the dust bowl. Over the years, Assaria has had several names, including Blackwolf and Oban.

The tiny town of Hedville had a few small businesses and a church but struggled to maintain its growth. The Great Depression was tough on the town, and the bank and the other few businesses there closed. Today, a grain elevator and the few buildings there are all that remain.

Smolan started as a small colony of Swedish settlers and was founded in 1886. The town has survived fires, tornados, and the rise and fall of Camp Phillips. The history is steeped in Swedish immigrants and their faith. Teacher and writer Tom Holmquist writes about the Swedish history of the area.

The town of Kipp also faced economic hardships during the Depression, and between fires and a huge tornado, it also faced the reality that the railroad did not give them a depot. So, one night in 1886, a group of men went to the neighboring town of Chico and stole the train depot right off the foundation and moved it on a railcar to Kipp.

The town of Salina, founded in 1858 by William Phillips, has boomed, and it remains the largest of the Saline County towns.

Glickville, Culver, Mentor, and Glendale all experienced the difficult times of the land, the Depression, and railroad decisions. Chico and Whitman's Corner, Oasis, and others no longer exist; they are merely shadows on the Saline County landscape. The land in Kansas was opened for settlement in 1854. Settlers flocked to the newly opened territories for their chance to own land and create new lives for themselves. The railroad had a huge influence on which towns made it and which did not. Weather, floods, tornados, fires, and economic disasters, as well as flour mills, gypsum mining, farming, and entrepreneurial spirit, created the Saline County of today. The history of Saline County is a reflection of the hardworking people and spirits that created it, forever immortalized in the images they leave behind.

One

EARLY SETTLERS AND COUNTY ORGANIZATION

Alex Adams and a woman and baby stand by the window of their Hedville, Kansas, home, while Fanny Spray stands in the doorway. Hedville is an unincorporated community in northern Ohio Township in Saline County. Hedville is on the Kansas & Oklahoma Railroad line, about one mile northwest of Salina. (CRKR.)

This tintype portrait shows Gotthart Schippel at age 35. He was one of the first settlers in Saline County, arriving in June 1857. He was born in Germany on May 6, 1835. He married Clara Wary in 1872, and they had nine children. Schippel rose to wealth, becoming the largest landholder and one of the wealthiest men in Kansas. One could not travel from Salina to New Cambria without stepping on his land. (CRKR.)

The Gotthart Schippel homestead was four miles northeast of Salina, and Schippel owned 6,000 acres of land. He sold hay and corn to the military. The house was built on the only dry land in the area, and a flood wiped out the government-built bridge in 1858. He was soon commissioned by the government to build and use a ferry for them, leading to his rise to wealth. (CRKR.)

Robert Parker was the third Saline County sheriff, from 1864 to 1865. The strife of the early battles with Native Americans over the land created a difficult job for Robert and his wife, Elizabeth. They had three children, John, Dora-Ann, and Evan. They left Saline County with their children to lead a quieter life in Sedan Township, Kansas. Robert passed away on March 6, 1899, and Elizabeth passed away on March 3, 1911. (CRKR.)

William and Anna Marie Boatman settled with their six children in the area of Glickville in 1873. Shown from left to right are Rebecca, Katharine, and Robert. Anna passed away in 1877 during childbirth. William married Margaret Miller, and she died shortly after the wedding. Margaret and three of the Boatman brothers are buried at the Sanborn Cemetery. (Courtesy of Janet Paradee.)

Ellen Nelson and Auntie Berg read in the parlor of their Hallville home in 1910. Hallville, Kansas, is a micro town southeast of Salina. (DWC.)

Nine unidentified men work in the fields of Bavaria using a threshing machine. Horses carry the processed grain. Bavaria, a town settled by the Swedish people, is also known by the earlier name of Hohneck. (DWC.)

Two

BAVARIA, FALUN, BROOKVILLE, AND TRENTON

A man rows a boat on Hall's Lake in Bavaria, Kansas, in 1890. As the area grew, the lake dried up due to changes in the water flow. (DWC.)

This photograph shows the various ages of students of the Bavaria High School class of 1927. Many of the boys are wearing coveralls, ready to resume their farm chores after school. Bavaria, also known as Hohneck, has always been a farming community. (DWC.)

The Bavaria railroad station is pictured from an eastward view in the late 1800s. (DWC.)

A steam train pulls into the Bavaria depot as the people wait for passengers to board. The town was built nine miles west of Salina on the line of the Kansas Pacific Railway. It was originally named Hohneck after Ernst Hohneck, who settled the area in 1865. In 1877, E.F. Drake had 25 acres of the east half of the town and renamed the area Bavaria. (DWC.)

A couple rows their boat on Hall's Lake in Bavaria, Kansas. A group of people stand watching on the shoreline. The lake dried up and is now farmland. (DWC.)

A group of workers surround the roller flour mill in Bavaria, Kansas. Roller flour mills were popular in Saline County in the late 1800s because they produced superior grain flour. The towns depended on the mills to process their grains. (DWC.)

This 1890 view from below Spring Creek Bridge in Bavaria, Kansas, shows what the town looked like at that time. Bavaria had several small businesses, including a syrup factory operated by Denton and Giessler. There was also a boardinghouse kept by Mrs. S. Terry. (DWC.)

Parishioners pose for a picture in front of the Bavaria church in the 1890s. Most of the children are kneeling in the first row. (DWC.)

The town stands in front of the Bavaria schoolhouse around 1886. The men are in top hats, and the ladies are in their Sunday-finest dresses. Bavaria has a proud history of Swedish immigration and farm culture. It had a general store that was operated by John Giessler, who also ran the lumberyard and the coal yard. (DWC.)

A man looks into the street from the front door of Joselyn's general store in Bavaria, Kansas, around 1890. Note the telephone pole leaning towards the building. (DWC.)

A large family stands in front of Terry's blacksmith shop in Bavaria in 1890. Piles of tractor and machine parts are scattered around the shop. The building is no longer there. (DWC.)

The shelves are stocked and full at Joselyn's general store in 1890. Bavaria's population grew quickly as waves of immigrants from Sweden came to find work and opportunity in Kansas. The Lutheran Church was instrumental in the growth, providing spiritual support to those who settled in the area. (DWC.)

A man and woman work in Joselyn's general store in 1890. The store shows the prosperity of the late 1890s in Bavaria as the train continued to bring in new settlers. (DWC.)

The people of the town stand in the middle of the street in Bavaria. The town was developed on the railway lines nine miles west of Salina, and the original town name was Hohneck. (DWC.)

A bicycle leans against the front of the post office in Bavaria. C.S. Joselyn was the postmaster there from 1886 to 1896. (DWC.)

Buggies and carriages are parked in front of Joselyn's general store in Bavaria. People stand in the street, all lined up for the photograph. (DWC.)

Lots of canned goods fill the shelves of Joselyn's general store in Bavaria. The clerk at the counter stands by rolls of wrapping paper, which were used to wrap purchases. (DWC.)

Hunters display their kill in a coyote roundup in 1913. Like the fox hunts of Europe, coyote roundups would bring the men out for the competition of the hunt. Coyotes posed problems for the farmers and their livestock, particularly their chickens and smaller animals. The coyote fur was also used for clothing. (DWC.)

While the townspeople cheer them on, the Bavaria baseball team plays against Hedville's team, the Mulberry Cow Punchers, in the late 1800s. Hedville's star pitcher was Joe Fonck. Baseball was an important pastime in Kansas, drawing large crowds that would pay to see the games. (DWC.)

The unique perspective of a bird's-eye view is the height of the camera, breaking-edge technology for the late 1800s. Bavaria had sustained growth because immigrants and other settlers were attracted to the area. (DWC.)

Third St., Falun, Kan.

This 1900 postcard of Third Street in Falun, Kansas, shows a drawing of the bank corner, third building from left, and the mercantile on the far right. The church can be seen in the background on the right. Many doctors settled in the town of Falun. The bank building is still there and is now used for community events. (Authors' collection.)

Falun State Bank, Falun, Kan.

The Great Depression, the dust bowl, and Camp Phillips all contributed to the downfall of Falun over the years. Camp Phillips, a military training base, led to the demise of most of Falun because of the drain on the economy. Businesses closed because the government was buying out the rural towns to grow Camp Phillips. This postcard of the Falun State Bank highlights the growth prior to the decline of the town. (Authors' collection.)

In 1887, Peter Soderburgh and Gustav Johnson built the Falun Public School building on Johnson's farm in District Seven of Saline County for a cost of $3,285. It was moved to the south part of Falun in 1889. This 1902 postcard shows how it looked in south Falun. (Authors' collection.)

There was a lot of activity at the Falun train depot in 1919. The railroad was instrumental in the growth of Falun. Livestock and feed were transported to and from the farms. Farmers would ship both their grains and milled flours to other communities through the trains. (Courtesy of Tom Holmquist.)

The Falun High School basketball team sits in the field with the parsonage behind them. Important to the communities, rural sports were watched by the townspeople and inspired intense rivalries. Today, the parsonage is surrounded by trees. (Courtesy of Tom Holmquist.)

Pictured looking south from Farmer's Union Elevator in 1921, one can see the G.A. Forsse Mill, the stockyard (in front of the mill), and a bird's-eye view of downtown Falun. The train tracks run by the elevator, and the small train depot is on the far right of the photograph. (DWC.)

Baseball was the national pastime of America prior to War World I. The ball field was just north of Falun on Fred Peterson's land. Sunday afternoons drew large crowds, and the admission price for adults was 25¢. Falun's baseball team won several titles over the years, including the Saline County championship. It frequently went up against the Salemburg baseball team, and its main competitor was the Salina Millers professional team. Good sportsmanship and fair play were important and stressed at this time. Unfortunately, the baseball spirit has been replaced by other activities over the years, and there is no longer a team. (DWC.)

Swedish immigrant G.A. Forsse joined other early settlers in this area in 1869. Supplies were hard to get, and the settlers would walk daily from Salina for 20 miles to get and sell their goods. This area was originally covered in bison, but they disappeared after the settlers took over the area. This 1920 view of Main Street in Falun looks south. (DWC.)

The stove dominates the interior room of the G.A. Forsse Flour Mill as four unidentified men do their work. Flour and grain created a dusty work space.

Brookville Grade School was situated at the center of town. The two-and-a-half-story, brown sandstone structure was built in 1875. The building was added onto in 1914. Today, it is used as both a hotel and apartments. It was built by Kruger and Parker on Jewett and Anderson Streets and is listed in the National Register of Historic Places. (DWC.)

The Brookville baseball team is pictured in 1912. The unidentified players competed against Glendale, Bavaria, and Falun. Since baseball was a serious pastime and sport, every town in Saline County had a team. (DWC.)

The Brookville marching band plays during the town fair next to the Brookville Hotel, which is on the corner. The Ringling Bros. Circus came to town in September 1908, as advertised on the sign on the building, which is on Anderson and Perry Streets. Note the boardwalk, which burned in a 1912 fire. (DWC.)

Four unidentified people stand out front of a regal old home in Brookville, Kansas, around 1910. Today, Brookville continues to support a population of about 250 people. It has become mostly a bedroom community to Salina commuters. Much of the town looks like it did when it was first developed, although the Brookville Hotel has been partially dismantled and no longer serves their famous chicken dinners. (DWC.)

Brookville Kubienecka Blacksmith and Works fixed carriage wheels in the late 1800s, when Brookville was a cattle town. During the cattle drives, the town would be full of cowboys and their livestock. Today, the building is an automotive shop. (DWC.)

This Brookville Elementary School class photograph shows a group of children in their overalls and best dresses. Today, the schoolhouse is an apartment. The young boys are wearing their nice hats, which are typical of the late 1800s. (DWC.)

Two unidentified men are photographed in front of a sandstone building. Brookville was famous for this style of brown sand brick. The building that is pictured housed an attorney's office that was split with a bank. Brookville got its start when the tracks of the Kansas Pacific Railroad reached the area in 1867. (DWC.)

This 1911 class photographs shows 17 unidentified high school students and teachers at Brookville School. The school was considered to be superior to many larger city schools in its design and structure. The beautiful, old stone school was last used as a grade school in 1996; it provided more than a 100 years of service. (DWC.)

Pictured here is a street view of the Brookville Hotel and opera house in the 1880s. However, Brookville's heyday was beginning to decline by the 1880s, and when the railroad relocated its roundhouse to Junction City in 1889, it nearly spelled a death knell for the city. Although only about 280 people called Brookville home by the turn of the century, it still supported a bank, newspaper, and post office, as well as a few other businesses. (DWC.)

Main and Second Streets are pictured in 1873. During the 1870s, Brookville peaked with a population of about 800 people. During this time, the town boasted a furniture store, hardware store, jewelry store, boot and shoe store, drugstore, tobacco store, millinery, wagon shop, livery stable, restaurant, and flour mill, as well as four general merchandise stores, one elevator, two hotels, and two lumberyards. (DWC.)

35

An interior view of the Brookville Sondergard Mercantile store is pictured here. Brookville was known as a lively town of enterprising people. Within the first year of the town's development, Brookville was attacked by Native Americans. Angered that the railroad was pushing west into their hunting grounds, a large group of warriors converged upon the town. The people of Brookville escaped to the roundhouse, where a barricade was hastily built for protection. (DWC.)

Brookville was the last station west of Salina on the Kansas Pacific Railway, making it an important cattle shipping point as cattle were driven northward from the Indian territories to the Chisholm Trail to be loaded on freight cars headed east. Since the railroad had granted the right-of-way for the town, it tried to impose a law that prohibited liquor in the city limits. However, this failed because saloonkeepers violated the restriction in order to serve the cowboys. (DWC.)

Pictured is a west-looking view of Brookville's Main Street in 1890. Brookville is located in Saline County, about 15 miles southwest of Salina. It is a shady little town with several handsome old buildings, including the Brookville Hotel. The first store in town was operated by George Snyder. M.P. Wyman put up the first house in town. (DWC.)

The Palace Restaurant in Brookville started in the 1890s and is at 11 Anderson Street in Brookville. Businesses came and went in town as the main industry was farming. Cattle were also an important industry there. (DWC.)

In the 1890s, Brookville Lutheran Church was located 15 miles southwest of Salina. Brookville's first settler was a man named John Crittenden. The first buildings erected in the town were the roundhouse and shops of the Kansas Pacific Railroad. (DWC.)

The Brookville City Hall and opera house burned down in the fire of 1905. The fire was devastating to the town, as it lost revenue from the cowboys on cattle runs. Brookville would continue to battle droughts, floods, other fires, and tornados over the years and survive it all, only to face economic setbacks during the Great Depression and later with a changing modernization of farming and cattle movement. (DWC.)

The Brookville Coronet Band plays outside of the opera house in the 1920s. Men with famous names visited Brookville in the frontier days. In 1871, Jesse and Frank James and their cousins the Ford boys camped there. Brookville was a typical cattle town. "Buffalo Bill" Cody and other notables of the pioneer days were in Brookville in the 1860s and later. (DWC.)

Brookville's city office and opera house are pictured in 1891. The town was laid out and surveyed by the Kansas Pacific Railway in April 1870. In June 1870, the railroad made big additions to the tracks and depot. The roundhouse was among the first buildings in town and created rapid growth. It was at the end of a road and attracted a good deal of people. John Crittenden was the first settler in Brookville, and the first mayor was William Brownhill. (DWC.)

Carlin Drug and Mercantile was one of the early stores in Brookville. George Snyder opened the first store in 1870 in the center of town, and the land office was located on the northwest corner of Anderson and Perry Streets. The first settlers of the town were mostly Civil War veterans and railroad men who were attracted to Brookville because it was a division point of the Kansas Pacific Railroad. (DWC.)

During World War II, the Brookville Hotel became even more famous as thousands of soldiers traveled from nearby Camp Phillips and the Smoky Hill Air Base. But when the war ended and Interstate Highways 70 and 135 were built near Salina, the town went into decline again. Still, the Brookville Hotel restaurant hung on at least until the year 2000. Though the old building still stands in Brookville, the restaurant itself moved to Abilene. (Authors' collection.)

40

Travelers enjoy the landscape of Brookville and the surrounding country. Visitors to the Brookville Hotel included Kansas governors and Old West icons, like Buffalo Bill, who signed the guest register. The topography includes several points of interest, including the Devil's Backbone, which is a line of hills. To the west of town is Horse Thief Canyon, famous as a hiding place for outlaws during the earlier lawless days. US Highway 40 that runs through Brookville is the old Butterfield Trail that connected Brookville to Salina and Abilene in 1865–1866. (Both, authors' collection.)

In 1968, the Brookville Hotel had 23 rooms. When the hotel first opened, the rate for a room was $1 for one night. KS-140 used to be US 40, an early transcontinental thoroughfare and predecessor to Interstate 70. Back roads going south out of Brookville tend to be blocked by the Air Force gunnery range. (Authors' collection.)

The Brookville Hotel was constructed in 1870. For decades, it was famous for its family-style fried chicken dinners until the family-owned restaurant relocated in 2000 to Abilene, where a replica Brookville Hotel was constructed. The original 143-year-old hotel was recently delisted from the National Register of Historic Places after state preservation officials determined that a recent renovation had negatively affected the historic integrity of the building. (Authors' collection.)

This 1964 Brookville Hotel postcard shows the dining room where its famous home-style chicken dinners were served family style. Today, the restaurant is in Abilene, Kansas, and it continues to serve the same menu. (Authors' collection.)

This 1964 postcard of the Brookville Hotel's dining room shows the hotel during its prime years. The hotel is no longer in the National Register of Historic Places, but the structure still stands in its original spot in Brookville. (Authors' collection.)

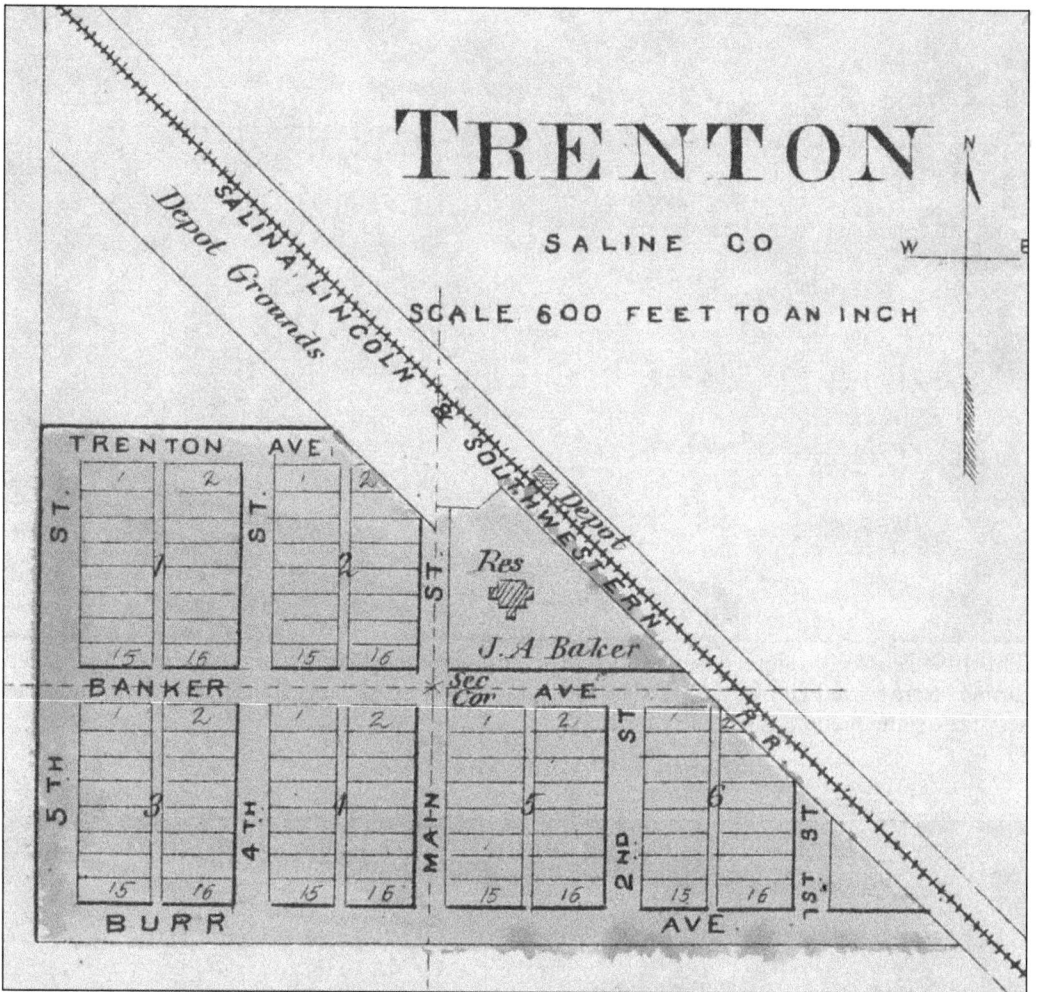

This 1884 Edwards Atlas map shows the small town of Trenton, which was established in 1884 by W.H. Banker, J.H. Banker, and Henry Burr. It was never really a town though, as no lots or land were sold. There was a horse ranch there for many years. (Authors' collection.)

Three

Bridgeport, Glickville, New Cambria, and Lightville

The Bridgeport School District 79 schoolhouse was the first building erected in Bridgeport in 1879. This 1905 photograph was taken at the southeast corner of Walnut and Third Streets. The school was later used as a home and a post office, and the building still stands today. (DWC.)

Main Street running through Bridgeport is pictured in 1908. Bridgeport, founded in 1879, was purchased from Sarah Husted for $500. The town company included president John Lamer and secretary J.C. Lamer. The town was named for the bridge over the Smoky Hill River, which was the only bridge between Lindsborg and Salina. Daniel Hawkins was an early settler of Bridgeport, and he had a dugout on the Smoky Hill River. (DWC.)

The graduates of the Bridgeport School are pictured on May 22, 1927. In 1879, John Hopkins and John Lamer built a water-powered mill; it stood until it was torn down in 1934. (DWC.)

In 1867, a colony of Swedes bought 2,000 acres of land in the Bridgeport area, and as soon as anyone not of their nationality moved in, the Swedes would buy them out. Wheat farming is the main industry of the area. When the Peck Cheese Factory was in operation, Bridgeport came to be known as the cheese capital of Kansas. (CRKR.)

The Bridgeport School, pictured in 1910, shows the progress of the community prior to the Great Depression and wars of the early 20th century. (DWC.)

An unidentified Bridgeport school building is pictured in the 1890s. The first school was built in 1881 on the northeast corner of Section 16, the road between Salina and Bridgeport, and classes were taught by Robert L. Cochran. It has since been replaced by a new building and has two teachers. (DWC.)

Bank of Hope Ministry Church in Bridgeport is pictured in 1902. The first church was organized in 1881 by the Presbyterians and, upon the disbanding of the Presbyterian Church, was purchased by the Methodist Episcopal Church. Bertha McKeever took the place of her husband, Rev. L.A. McKeever, whose death happened suddenly. (DWC.)

Bridgeport schoolchildren sit in a wagon in 1918. When the railroad was built in 1879, an elevator was erected and wagon trains were often more than a half-mile long to get to the elevators. The town was growing and in need of schools. (DWC.)

The Bridgeport flood in the 1940s devastated the area. When the railroad was built in 1879, the train went from Hutchinson to Salina. The area was like a bowl after the construction of the railroad, which made the land prone to flooding. Because it was built in the wrong area, the train coming through actually killed the town. (Gutka Collection.)

The Bridgeport flood in the 1940s was representative of the power of the storms that would come through Saline County. Droughts alternated with heavy rains, causing problems for the farmlands and towns. The US government started a Soil Bank program to replace grasslands and seed the pasturelands to help against floods. (Gutka Collection.)

The droughts and dust bowl years of the 1930s and the Bridgeport flood in the 1940s took their toll on the land. Over farming, modern equipment, and topsoil losses created problems for the farmlands. Many floods occurred in the 1940s, destroying towns and wiping out the land. (Gutka Collection.)

The Dairy Maple and Benfield Bridge was removed when the New Cambria Mill was torn down in the 1930s. The bridge flooded often as the dam downstream would overflow due to improper construction, causing problems for the residents in the area and the mill.

Cambria Mills, owned by Simon P. Donmyer, was considered the best mill in Kansas for its time. It was built in 1885 and managed by William R. Geis and Edward H. Gibbs. There was also a mercantile store inside the mill. Farmers would hold meetings on the third floor of the mill, which was located in Glickville. This 1910 photograph shows the mill already in some disrepair. (Courtesy of the Saline County Native Daughters Collection.)

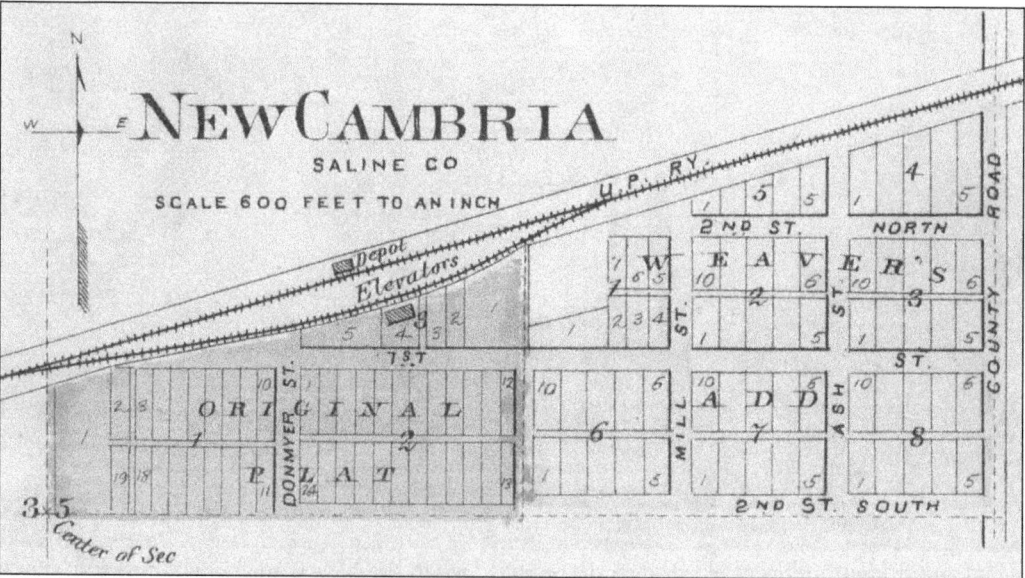

This map of New Cambria from the Edwards Atlas Map of Saline County shows the settlement plan in 1874.

The New Cambria State Bank opened in January 1890 and closed after a fire on September 26, 1927. This was during the era of drought in Kansas. Overproduction stimulated by the demands of World War I and the development of gas-fueled tractors created difficult financial times. (Authors' collection.)

New Cambria School was built during the era known as Kansas's Settlement and Organization, an era that represented rapid growth from 1870 to 1900 and a time of immigration, homestead claims, home building, and farm development. New Cambria School house was built in 1887 during a time of rapid growth in Saline County. The school was built by the Swedish settlers of the area who were flocking to Kansas for farming opportunities and homesteads. Bad weather, insects, crop failures, and national financial depressions plagued this era as well. (CRKR.)

New Cambria School Room No. 2, pictured in 1908, was one of the early country schools that served the community. The period from 1900 to 1920, through World War I, was described as the era that population peaked for Saline County. It seemed a time of inflation, with greater returns reaped from land and livestock compared to the previous meager years. Cars replaced horses, and steam engines provided threshing machine power. World War I also brought a higher demand for wheat. (CRKR.)

New Cambria Hotel was one of the early enterprises of the town. The Saline County Atlas of 1884 described New Cambria as a "place of considerable business, surrounded with finely cultivated farms. It has one store, one grain elevator, one hotel, blacksmith shop and schoolhouse and especially noticeable is the handsome stone depot and store." (CRKR.)

54

The New Cambria train depot was made of stone and built in 1884. Gotthard Schippel, who procured the government land, originally settled Cambria, later called New Cambria. He proved up the claim, and the land is still in possession of his heirs. At this time, Kansas was still a disputed territory, inhabited by Native Americans and wild animals. The government engineers had just completed a rough bridge across the Saline River and left a cabin, which Schippel took over. (CRKR.)

New Cambria's Donmyer Building was constructed in 1886, and it burned down in 1896. Fires proved to be catastrophic to the wooden structures of the time. The early settlers soon learned that Kansas's fickle weather was also a problem for wooden structures. Although sandstone, brownstone, brick, and other stones were more desirable building materials, they were difficult to get until the trains became more active. (CRKR.)

Four

ASSARIA, GYPSUM, MENTOR, AND HEDVILLE

Assaria had an initial population of 56 people. It was founded in 1886 by Mans Peterson and Ben Hisser. In 1879, Highland Fairchild of the Town Company organized and laid out the town. In 1883, Assaria was a booming town with a roller mill that produced several thousand barrels of flour a week. In the late 1950s, Assaria put on a series of outdoor concerts that generated a lot of publicity. Oban, a Scottish word meaning "Little Bay," was the original name for the town. The Scottish settlers were not fond of the weather of Assaria and left the town in 1886. It sat empty until the Swedish people came along and discovered that they could produce flour there. Pictured is a map of Assaria from Edwards Atlas Map of Saline County of 1884. (Authors' collection.)

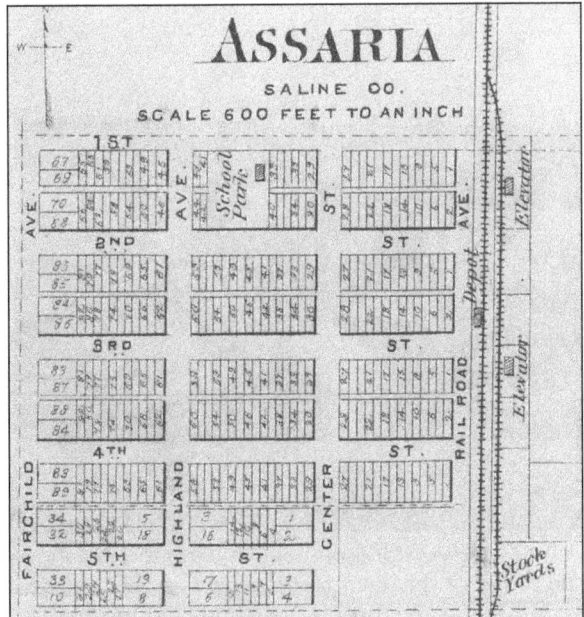

Assaria's Union Pacific train depot carried flour from the mill to Salina. Unidentified men load the train from a wagon. The flour roller mill is visible in the back of the image. (DWC.)

A bird's-eye view of downtown Assaria in 1892 shows the wooden boardwalk that runs through the center of the town past the livery stable. Boardwalks were a big improvement because they kept the mud and dirt off shoes and clothing, making the shops more accessible. (DWC.)

This west-looking photograph of Main Street in Assaria shows people driving horse-drawn carriages. An unidentified man and his dog stand in the center of the street. The horse-drawn carriage to the left of the photograph is in front of the hotel. Note the woman wearing a big hat and coat to the right of the photograph; she is dressed in the fashion of the times. (DWC.)

This October 1906 postcard of the schoolhouse in Assaria shows the quality of the workmanship of the time. The writing on the edge of the postcard states that there was time to make a stop to see the school. (CRKR.)

Assaria Swedish Lutheran Church had a single steeple and was made of wood. The Scottish settlers originally constructed this church, and when the Swedish took it over, they rebuilt to their own design standards. The Swedish were leery of wooden churches, as they burned on the prairie. They rebuilt this church out of brick. (CRKR.)

The hotel is at left in this photograph. There are lots of places to rest one's horse in downtown Assaria, and looking closely, one can see a man peeking out of the side dormer window of the hotel. (CRKR.)

The Assaria Lodge Room sits above the mercantile store, where the sign reads, "Star Brand Shoes are better." G.A. Frost owned the mercantile and building. (DWC.)

A distant view of Assaria Lutheran Church and its cemetery shows the single steeple made of wood. The church was later moved, but parts of the church's foundation remain. The cemetery surrounds it. (CRKR.)

Note the black top hat on the dapper gentleman as he stands proudly on the porch with an unidentified woman and child at the Assaria Swedish Lutheran Parsonage. The parsonage caught on fire and burned down, as did many wooden structures. (CRKR.)

Unidentified men, women, and children pose on the porch for pictures at the Assaria Hotel. The trees have no leaves, but the people are relaxed on the boardwalk. (CRKR.)

The Trojan basketball team and cheerleaders of 1960–1961 pose in this photograph. Pictured are (first row) Margie Hanson, Beth Larson, and Judy Magnuson; (second row) Tom Small, Dennis Lily, Clarence Howard, and two unidentified; (third row) Coach Randy McMurray, Roger Burkhead, Nike Holmes, Richard Shogren, Dennis McMurray, J. Beach, Merle Norman. (MC.)

64

Members of Assaria High School's theater arts program of 1959–1960 comprised the cast and crew of this production of *The Curious Savage*. (MC.)

Margie Hanson and Judy Magnuson perform in the play *The Curious Savage*. Written by John Patrick, it is a comedic play about Ethel P. Savage, a woman whose husband recently died and left her approximately $10 million. Contrasting the kindness and loyalty of psychiatric patients with the avarice and vanity of "respectable" public figures, it calls into question conventional definitions of sanity while lampooning celebrity culture. (MC.)

From left to right, Alice Schaffer, Kathy Ball, Judy Magnusson, unidentified, and Tom Small from Assaria High School's theater arts program perform *The Curious Savage*. The play was the highlight of the town's social calendar. The theater group produced three plays between the fall of 1959 and the spring of 1960. (MC.)

From left to right, Kathy Ball, Dennis Lily, and Ronite Fosberg Magnuson are pictured here. Dennis played the violin in Assaria High School's performance of *The Curious Savage*. The play explored the comedic ideas of what a person does with a large inheritance of $10 million and how greed can infect everyone involved. (CRKR.)

Judy Magnuson and Margie Hanson perform in *The Curious Savage*. High school theater productions were valued community events. (MC.)

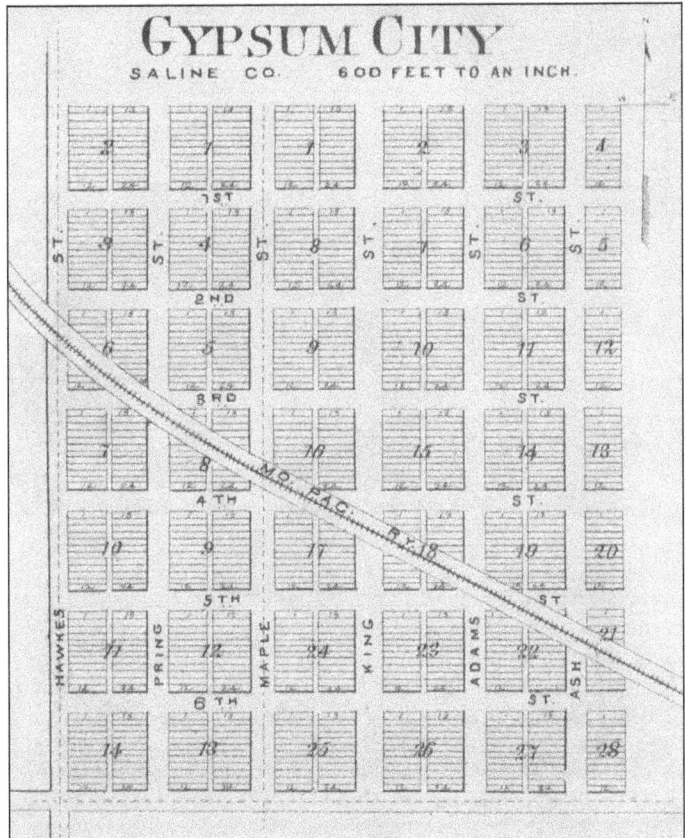

GYPSUM CITY

SALINE CO.   600 FEET TO AN INCH.

Pictured here is a map of Gypsum from when it was called Gypsum City. "Young Valley Queen" was an affectionate term that people used to describe the beautiful city that produced flours and grains. In 1887, Jonathan Tickler and John Kingman settled Gypsum on the newly built railroad line. In 1890, there were 530 people living in the town. (Authors' collection.)

An unidentified woman holds on to her umbrella in the wind in this photograph of downtown Gypsum from around 1900. The census of 2010 shows the city population at 405, down from the original 530 in 1890. (DWC.)

Gypsum's post office is pictured in 1909, after it was built by Johnathan Smitter on the corner of Schmitting and Manning Streets. The Gypsum Advocate printing store and newspaper was located here. At the time, Gypsum had over 10 newspapers, as did other towns such as Brookville, Kansas. They had the same news as the other papers, but that did not stop them from delivering their news. In the window to the right is a bicycle of the times. The building sat vacant from 1926 to 1946, was sold to Roy Manning, and was converted into the Kansan Theatre. The opening show at the theater was a comedy called *Gallant Best*. It was 39¢ for adults and 14¢ cents for children to attend. (CRKR.)

This 1932 photograph of the Gypsum public grade school shows the large number of children in the area. When the school opened in 1887, James Nash was the principal and there were 40 students. In the early 1890s, a second story was added to the building. A flood caused cracks in the wall and the building to become unsafe in 1896. The building was fixed, and a two-story west wing was added to the school in 1907. (CRKR.)

This postcard of Gypsum High School shows the two-story addition and the west wing. The school was both a high school and elementary school until 1978. The students went to a different school for intermediate classes from 1927 to 1978. (Authors' collection.)

The First Baptist Church of Gypsum held its first worship services in rural schools and community buildings. The church itself was built in 1904, and the Reverend Stitts was the first to lead the congregation of the church. The church has gone through many renovations over the years, and stairs and doors have been added as more parishioners joined. (Authors' collection.)

The Akers Building in Gypsum contained T.H. Rubin Hardware, F.R. Higgins Medicine and Dental Co., and the Gypsum Co-operative Store. Akers purchased the building on the east side of Baker Street in 1908. The building also housed a bowling alley, clothing store, and several bakeries. (CRKR.)

The Gypsum flour mill and elevator are featured in this 1908 postcard from Teichgraeber Milling Company. In the spring of 1887, the mill was discussed in hopes that it would allow the town to grow and benefit from the surrounding farms. The mill was planned in 1889 and built that year. In 1890, the mill was an expert flour roller mill. By 1910, Phillip Teichgraeber had sold his interest in the mill, and the name was changed to the Gypsum City Mill. (Authors' collection.)

Gypsum Public School was closed in 1978, and the students were moved to another school building outside of Gypsum. The school building went through many changes over the years, and it now sits abandoned and surrounded by trees. (Authors' collection.)

Gypsum is pictured during a flood on January 12, 1910. Since the late 1800s, Gypsum has had a history of floods, most of which were considered to be nuisances and ultimately did not do too much damage. However, a major flood hit Gypsum in 1903 and did considerable damage. In late January 1910, the eastern portion of Gypsum flooded and the temperatures dropped, leaving four inches of ice. Dikes were built after that in an effort to control future flooding. In this photograph, one can see the ice around the trees that formed overnight after it flooded. (CRKR.)

In Gypsum, the Suitatorium was the place to buy clothes. Six men pose in their coveralls as they wait for a shave and haircut outside of McFarland Barbershop. Located at 521 Maple Street, the barbershop opened in 1913 and closed in 1920. From left to right are customers T.M. Miller, Samuel Madams, and Jim Sutton; barbers Clyde McFarland and Joe Sneider; and an unidentified boy, who was an assistant. (MC.)

Gypsum military men stand in front of the bakery. The mayor of Gypsum hired Fort Riley troops, who brought down cannon that they used against Brookville in an earlier battle in 1872. The two towns did not care for each other, and disputes were frequent because they were in competition for the railroad depot. The military men and hired Native Americans pointed the cannon towards Brookville in a show of defiance, and Gypsum lost the battle. (MC.)

The office of the *Gypsum Banner* served the important purpose of documenting community events. F.E. Gamble was the editor of the newspaper. The first issue came out on April 9, 1886, before the town became incorporated as a town. The building pictured here in 1886 was originally from Chico, a dismantled town. (CRKR.)

The Bickle Ranch was three miles north of Gypsum and one mile west of Chico in 1886. Ranching, cattle, and grain were the staples of the economy at this time. Saline County's growth remained steady as the cowboys continued to drive cattle through the trails and to the train depots that carried it to the East Coast. (CRKR.)

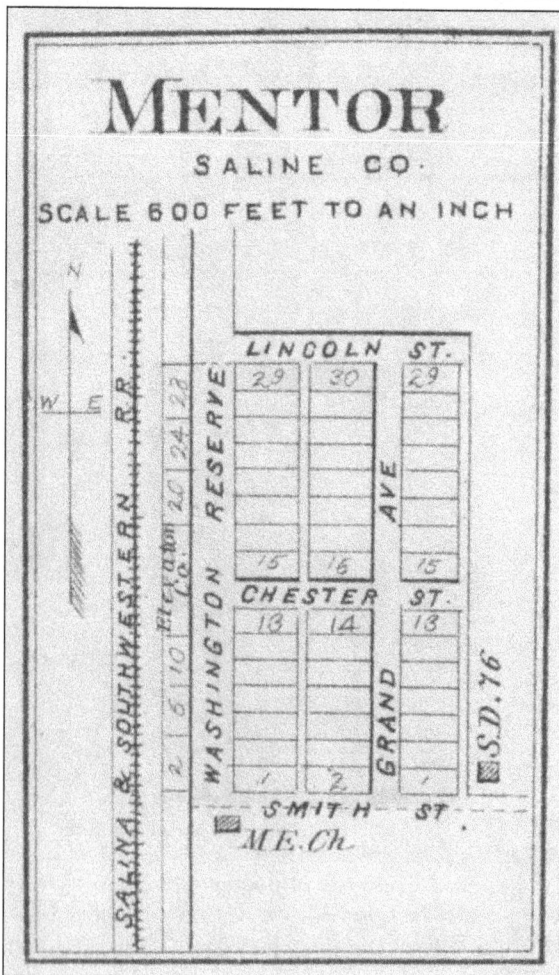

Mentor started out of a tiny settlement called Pleasant Ridge in the 1860s. As early as 1886, there was a Methodist church there, and a railroad was built through the area in 1883 that went as far as Pleasant Ridge. Authorities thought that too many towns in Kansas had similar names, so they changed the name of the town to Mentor. Soon, Mentor had a hotel, blacksmith shop, store, and other small businesses. After 1919, the town of Mentor was sold. Today, it is still called Mentor but is now located at the southwest edge of Salina. (Authors' collection.)

Children play outside the Mentor Elementary School, which was built in 1883. This schoolhouse was also used as a church, which was common for this time period as buildings needed to be able to handle many community functions. (CRKR.)

The Methodist church in Mentor, pictured here in 1875, was also used as a school. It was active until it was torn down 1919. A brick church replaced this building. (CRKR.)

Hedville Marching Band is pictured here in 1903. From left to right are (first row) Art Sampson, Henry Engstrom, Axel Hedquist, Fred Oberg, Leonard Thelander, and Rudolph Shublosom; (second row) Elmer Hedquist, Leonard Tilberg, Vic Oberg, Albin Tilberg, August Johnson, and Phillip Marines. As of 1968, Rudoph Shublosom was the only surviving member of this group. Axel and Elmer Hedquist were the town founders. (Authors' collection.)

Five

KIPP, SMOLAN, AND CAMP PHILLIPS

Kipp Retail Shop started a few miles northwest of Chico in a town called Kipp. It was named after a Missouri Pacific Railroad master. After a year of fighting with Kipp over the rights to a railroad depot, the railroad in Chico closed in 1894. (CRKR.)

Gustave Johnson General Merchandise store is pictured in 1890. The town of Kipp struggled to survive over the years, and the town was on a major decline by time of the Great Depression. (CRKR.)

Chico men fight to save their railroad depot from the men of Kipp. The depot was moved to Kipp overnight, causing many problems for Chico. Kipp also began to decline when the depot was burned in 1934. In June 1943, a tornado destroyed many of the buildings that were moved from Chico to Kipp. (CRKR.)

78

Though the building that originally housed Kipp Mercantile, pictured here in 1913, was from Chico, it was relocated to Kipp after the railroad depot was stolen from Chico. Businesses relocated closer to the new depot stop in Kipp. (CRKR.)

William Exline, the founder of the town of Kipp, built Kipp Exline Shop in 1886. Exline Diesel Company was the largest engine shop in Kansas. Kipp had a few homes, and for the town to have a chance, they needed a railroad. The nearby town of Chico had a depot, so in 1886, a group of men from Kipp raised the Chico depot off its foundation, put it on a railroad car, and stole the depot. Eventually, when the town of Chico died, the houses in Chico were moved to the Kipp area. In the 1950s, Exline moved to Salina. (CRKR.)

Kipp High School cheerleaders are pictured here in 1924. In 1929, Kipp passed a $55,000 bond (which they are still paying off) that was issued for a full-service school with the largest gym in Saline County. The high school burned down in 1953, and another was built but closed in the 1960s. (CRKR.)

Kipp Consolidated School is pictured in 1927. The last school in Kipp closed in 1978. (CRKR.)

The Smolan area was first settled when a group of 75 Swedes bought 20,000 acres from the Kansas Pacific Railroad. Later, 60 more Swedes from Galesburg, Illinois, relocated to the area. In 1886, the Missouri Pacific Railroad laid a track through the area, and John Danielson plotted 20 acres for the townsite. Within a short time, there was a store, a post office, and an elevator. The growth was rapid, and within a few years, there were a number of businesses and a hotel. The town of Smolan is pictured here in 1908. (Authors' collection.)

Construction started on Smolan Bank after the tornado, and it opened in 1917. (CRKR.)

A tornado struck Smolan in April 1892. Smolan has higher-than-average tornado activity compared to many other Kansas towns. Tragedy struck when the tornado destroyed a large part of Smolan. The town refused to die, so the telephone service came to town and created more opportunities for the community in 1896. (Courtesy of Tom Holmquist.)

E.P. Karleen was the pastor of Smolan Lutheran Church. In 1869, a number of Swedes came from Illinois, including founder J.M. Danielson, who also helped with Salemsburg Lutheran Church. On August 3, 1893, Smolan Lutheran Church was founded when two congregations came into one church, as a group had migrated from Salemsborg's congregation. The church was dismantled in 1919, and the bell was moved later to the Salemsborg church. (Courtesy of Tom Holmquist.)

LUTHERAN CHURCH, SMOLAN, KANS.

This postcard shows Third Street in Smolan, Kansas. A major fire burned down Smolan's two general stores in 1924, but the townspeople rebuilt them. In 1926, a high school was built in Smolan at a cost of $20,000; it closed in 1950. The school is now a restaurant. (Courtesy of Tom Holmquist.)

THIRD STREET, SMOLAN, KANSAS.

Greetings from CAMP PHILLIPS

SALINA, KANSAS

According to the Kansas Historical Society, Camp Phillips was a large-scale military training camp that grew to cover 46,000 acres and housed 75,000 to 80,000 soldiers at one time. Designed in 1943 to be a five-year camp, it also served as a POW camp for 3,000 Germans and Italians. That summer, Smolan swelled from a town of about 100 people to over 1,000. Smolan high school students, enticed by good wages, took jobs helping the government survey the land. (Courtesy of Tom Holmquist.)

According to www.808th.com military records of Camp Phillips, almost overnight, Smolan residents watched their city being turned into a camp town that rested on the rim of a military base 350 times greater than itself. Yet 143 farm families felt an even greater impact when they were told their land was being secured by the government and they would have to relocate. (Courtesy of Tom Holmquist.)

In the midst of these inconvenient, over-crowded conditions, new Smolan businesses sprang up. Once accustomed to serving only a few farmers and residents, the city of Smolan soon shifted its activities to serve construction and military needs as well. Florence Oborg operated her café in the basement of the brick building on Main Street. Fresh water was carried from the gas station daily. Three oil stoves were used to cook 150 meals a day. Added to this was the chore of carrying dirty dishwater out of the basement. At that time, Smolan also had a drugstore, clothing shop, two or three grocery stores, and three other cafés. A tent served as a temporary movie theater. (Courtesy of Tom Holmquist.)

Soldiers relax in the grass while watching a gun demonstration. While some farmers sought other land to buy after theirs was taken, others left farming entirely. Those who left farming were given little time, often less than a month, to search for a place to move. As the camp neared completion, there was an exodus of workers. Tracks carried troop trains and cars filled with POWs. The days of camp-town frenzy, when prisoners escaped or wandered off, came to a close three months after World War II ended in 1945. The camp was moved to the new Schilling Air Force Base. (Courtesy of Tom Holmquist.)

Six

SALEMSBORG, HALLVILLE, GLENDALE, AND CULVER

According to www.lutheransonline. com, "This August 1925 image shows Evangelical Salemsburg Lutheran Church on Route One in Smolan, Kansas. Salemsborg, which means 'Peaceful Fortress,' was founded in the summer of 1869, and within a few years, the valley was filled with farms and businesses where Swedish language and culture, art and music, and Swedish Lutheranism would flourish. The first church building was made of sod. Members of many of the same families, back to the original immigrants, are laid to rest at the cemetery here. There are also many graves of the same name, although not of the same families, interred close to one another throughout the cemetery." (Courtesy of Tom Holmquist.)

This 1927 image shows the Salemsborg Church burning. The Salemsborg Church has a compelling story. It started as a sod church in 1869, half buried in the ground. People had to stand in the mud to worship, and sometimes they got stuck to the floor. A classic frame church was built in 1874, but it was replaced by a magnificent spire church that was 46 meters (152 feet) tall in 1893. This was one of the tallest Lutheran churches in Kansas. On July 25, 1925, the spire was hit by lightning. Frantic efforts to cut the spire loose to save the church were futile given the available tools. People rushed into the burning edifice with a hay wagon and managed to pry the large altar painting off the wall and save it, along with the electric motor of the organ. The church burned to ashes in about an hour and a half. In 1926, the church was rebuilt, and it remains in wonderful condition with stunning stained-glass windows imported from Germany. The painting that was saved from the fire is still above the altar. (Courtesy of Tom Holmquist.)

In the summer of 1868, Anders W. Dahlsten, pastor of the First Lutheran Church in Galesburg, led a party representing the Galesburg Land Company to Kansas to search for a place where a large group of Swedes could settle, find economic opportunity, retain their Swedish culture, and, most importantly, worship God in a free environment. The Swedes found that place in the Smoky Valley of central Kansas. (Courtesy of Tom Holmquist.)

Alfred Mattson stands in the center of this 1910 photograph. He worked for Emil Carlson, the first proprietor of the general store. Several years later, Mattson went into business for himself. Hallville was named after Luther Hall, whose land was six miles south of Assaria. In 1887, Hall dug a well and stuck it into a vein of coal about 109 feet below the surface. Hallville became the name of the railroad station, although Wonderly was the name given to the post office, which was there before the railroad depot. (CRKR.)

Two young women hold their cats on a Hallville farm in the late 1800s. In 1890, Hallville was an area of good farming and grazing land, making it an ideal place for shipping cattle and wheat. The land was hard fought over in the railroad depot battles, as a depot could make or break an area. On February 24, 1887, a huge crowd of people from Lindsborg, Bridgeport, and Gypsum came to a meeting to determine where the train depot would be located; they felt that the Missouri Pacific Railroad Company had created rivalries with the town of Assaria. (CRKR.)

This bird's-eye view of Olson Mercantile shows the tiny village of Hallville, which was comprised of a grocery store, grain elevator, depot, and a section house that was furnished as living quarters for the railroad foreman and his family. The population was only about 10 people. Political rallies, family functions, and neighboring farms families would come to the village for holidays and weekends. (CRKR.)

A sod house in Glendale is pictured in 1920. Glendale was named after the landscape of the area of Mulberry Creek, which flows through a narrow valley through glens and dales. It is at an altitude of 1,400 feet and is on a branch of the Santa Fe Railroad. Founded in 1915, the first house in town was built on Second Street and is still in use today. The Glendale State Bank was built in 1916 and closed when the Depression hit in 1932. (CRKR.)

The last sod house in the Glendale area is pictured here. It is two miles east of Glendale, near the location where Etienne de Bourgmont's treaty with the Native Americans was negotiated in 1724, and is the oldest historic spot in Saline County. A tree known as the "Treat Tree" formerly shaded the site, but it was destroyed by a storm one spring day in 1869. The Salina Northern Railroad gave the town of Glendale its first transportation in 1915. The railroad was taken over by the Santa Fe Line in 1924. (CRKR.)

Within the photograph:

Edgar Reed
Coach

Louisa Holtz
Forward

Selma Matt
Guard

Lucille Fonck
Forward

Evalyn Daum
Center

Glendale Rural High School Basket Ball Team 1927
Glendale 547 • Opponents 215

Elsie Matt
Guard

Viola Lebert
Guard

Emma Jilka
Captain

Clara Haupt
Center

Ruth Rittgers
Forward

The 1927 women's basketball team of Glendale Rural High School is pictured here. From left to right are (top row) Louisa Holtz (forward), Selma Matt (guard), Edgar Reed (coach), Lucille Fonck (forward), and Evalyn Daum (center); (bottom row) Elsie Matt (guard), Viola Lebert (guard), Emma Jilka (captain), Clara Haupt (center), and Ruth Rittgers (forward). (CRKR.)

The Glendale High School basketball team is pictured in 1939. The rural high school building measured 60 by 90 feet and cost $13,000 to build in 1922. There were five teachers, and the high school had a band under the direction of Owen Cobb. (CRKR.)

A member of Glendale High School's 1938 basketball team is pictured here. The school was part of School District 33. In Glendale, a small town with a population of 33, sports were a vital part of the community. Hunting and fishing were done in neighboring fields and streams. On the Charles Bueker farm, located three miles south of Glendale, is a cave containing Indian pictographs; it is the only site of Native American recorded history in the area. (CRKR.)

A member of Glendale High School's 1938 basketball team waves at the camera. The main industries in Glendale are raising cattle and winter wheat farming. The town has an elevator and general store, a hardware store, and garage. (CRKR.)

A player for Glendale High School's 1938 basketball team strikes a pose. In 1922, a consolidated school that measured 40 by 80 feet was built at a cost of $7,000. The town of Glendale is considered a micro town. Its Lutheran church was organized in 1917 and had a membership of 60. (CRKR.)

A basketball player from Glendale High School's 1938 team is pictured here. Glendale's students frequented Halloween parties about a mile out of town at the Henry Hotz farmhouse, which built out of stone by a stonecutter from Switzerland. Henry Hotz and his wife were also born in Switzerland. The house had two basements, one under the other, and the lower basement was a quarry. A flight of steps led to the first basement, and from there, another set of steps was cut in the sand rock down to a large basin hewn from soft sand rock. In the corner of the pit was a spring of water. It was dark and ghostly looking, making it a great place for parties. (CRKR.)

Main Street, Culver, Kansas.

This 1910 image shows Main Street in Culver, Kansas, only a few years before the fire of 1915 that burned down the hotel. Along with Hedville, Culver remains a center for livestock and grain. Culver has a train stop, critical for its survival. (Courtesy of Salina Public Library, Campbell Room of Kansas Research, Dale Weiss.)

Seven

EDUCATION AND RELIGION

Part of District One, the Schippel schoolhouse closed in May 1965 after 98 years of teaching local students. Alfreda Burton was the last teacher there. The classes typically held about 30 children. Declining enrollments closed many one-room schoolhouses in rural areas. This school opened on September 4, 1867. (CRKR.)

Crown Point KS Humbarger, School District 11, was located at Elm Creek Township; it was started in April 22, 1866. Schools at this time were created through a pooling of the town's resources and people. Many students read from tattered Bibles, and some were lucky enough to have McGuffey Readers. (CRKR.)

The Wheeler School, pictured here in 1890, was started in District 59 of the Liberty Township on November 27, 1875. It was one of two country schools in the area; the other was the Star School, two miles west of Hallville. Robert Wheeler owned the land across the road that was north of Wheeler School. The two schools had great sports and game rivalries. (CRKR.)

The town of Trenton, Kansas, was founded in 1886. Ebenezer School was in School District 29, located in Trenton, Kansas. The school was established shortly after the town was founded. The stove in the classroom burned both cow chips and wood. The school no longer exists. (CRKR.)

Sunny Slope School, located two miles from Smolan Kansas District 63, was started in February 1879. (CRKR.)

West Sunnyside School District 65, pictured in 1930, was organized on February 24, 1879. When a new schoolhouse was built in the southwest area of the township in 1913, the first schoolhouse was sold for $57. In 1924, the school building was remodeled and enlarged with a basement at a cost of $2,430. The building was sold to the US government in 1942 and was later destroyed by a fire. The first teacher was Horace Jemerson and the last was Emma Crist. (CRKR.)

Sunny Corners School, of School District 37 in Smokey View Township, was established on March 28, 1872. The children play around while getting their photographs taken. (CRKR.)

On April 23, 1873, the Summit Hill School, located in Walnut Township, was established. The Walnut Township is east of Smolan, Kansas. The area includes many of the original farms of the Swedish immigrants. As of the 2000 census, there were 218 people, 79 households, and 63 families still residing in the area, representing very little population change from the late 1800s. (CRKR.)

Students stand for their pictures in Summit Hills School District 47 in Walnut Township. The Smolan area was first settled when a group of 75 Swedes bought 20,000 acres from the Kansas Pacific Railroad. Later, 60 more Swedes from Galesburg, Illinois, relocated to the area where many of the original families still live. (CRKR.)

Pohenta-Kipp School is pictured on graduation day in the 1930s. The first county school in Saline County started as a dugout on the banks of Old Dry Creek Stream. Organized in the spring of 1865, the school was named Gypsum. When a flood destroyed the school in 1867, it was moved to a log house owned by Galveston Taylor. The Pohenta school was organized on June 19, 1869. The school building was completed in November 1870. The school was a cultural and social center for the community of Pohenta, providing a space for Sunday school, church societies, and spelling bees. Mary Stockwell was the first teacher hired at Poheta. (Courtesy of Salina Public Library, Campbell Room of Kansas Research.)

The interior of Pliny School in District 29 is pictured here. The school was organized and opened on June 29, 1871. The first school sessions were held in the home of J.D. Marsh. Grace Hartmon, Beverly Hill, and Lily Bickle were some of the teachers. It later burned down. (CRKR.)

Pliny School opened in 1895 and closed in 1952. The school building was later sold to the Carlton Baptist Church in Carlton and used as their fellowship hall. (CRKR.)

Pleasant Hills School District 32 was built in 1872 and disbanded in 1940. The building was then used as a house. (Courtesy of Salina Public Library, Campbell Room of Kansas Research, Dale Weiss.)

Muir School District Six was located in the Smolan Township and organized on March 10, 1866. It was the sixth schoolhouse to be built in Saline County. The population of Smolan was very small, and the train was just being built through the area. (CRKR.)

Iron Mound School District 58, located in Greeley Township, was established on May 24, 1874. Some of the schoolchildren could not go to the New Cambria school because Simon Donmyer would not allow people who were not related to attend his school. (CRKR.)

Malmgren School District 20 was organized on March 19, 1940, and it became a part of District Seven on March 1, 1947. Susie Cooley was the school's first teacher. The building was constructed in 1917 and later sold at auction on May 1, 1947. It was then moved near Lindsborg, Kansas, and converted into a house. In 1991, there was a series of robberies in the county, and the robbers hid out in the renovated schoolhouse. They were gunned down in front of the schoolhouse. (CRKR.)

Magnolia School District 77, located in Smokey Hill Township in the city of Salina, opened on June 25, 1883. At the time, the one-room schoolhouses taught students of every age. Students had inconsistent educations due to the expansion of the frontier and constant movement of the people. (CRKR.)

Lightville School, School District 19, was located in Lightville, Kansas, in the Ohio Township, and it started March 16, 1870. The town was created by the Kansas Missouri Railroad Company, but it was so close to other prominent railroad depots, including Bavaria, that it was not successful. Lightville no longer exists, but a road bearing its name is in Salina. (DWC.)

Falun Englund School house in School District 60 was built in 1898 on the southeast corner of the Washington Township at a cost of $725. In 1917, it was temporarily moved so that a basement could be built under it. In 1922, the US government sold the school building for $1,750, and the contents of the school sold for $302. The first school teacher who served at the school was Fanny McGratney, and she was there for four months. The last teacher was Linnea Olson. (CRKR.)

Carlson School, Washington Township, in School District 70, started on February 1879. Children would take their lunches to school wrapped in cloth or in old pails. Many schools of this time period had dirt floors. (CRKR.)

The Schippel School house in 1884 was located in the Cambria Township, District 3, and organized on September 4, 1867. Schippel's Ferry brought in many new people to the community, thereby accelerating the growth of Salina and Saline Counties as people came in waves after the Civil War. (CRKR.)

The Lockard School was located in Elm Creek Township, District 7, and opened on May 7, 1866. While some areas were experiencing rapid growth, others were not, which led to inconsistent educational standards in schools of this time period. Textbooks were also an issue because while some children had McGuffey Readers, others learned to read from Bibles or slates, depending on the resources of the towns. (CRKR.)

The town of Culver was named after George Culver, who was killed while volunteering during a conflict with Native Americans at the Battle of Arickaree on the Colorado and Kansas border. Sustained growth occurred after the railroad arrived in 1886, and Culver remained an important trading town until after World War I. The Culver Bank closed and moved, causing the decline of the town. Culver High School, pictured here, remains standing, but the building is now a community hall. (CRKR.)

Smolan basketball team is, from left to right, (sitting) Norley, R. Holmquist, and G.S. Wedenberg; (standing) Coach Panter, Nabey, Ralph Anderson, Ehet Anderson, Danielson, and unidentified. (CRKR.)

The Smolan High School girls' basketball team of 1927–1928 consisted of, from left to right, (first row) five unidentified; (second row) Annie Holmquist, Helen Anderson, unidentified, and Evelgu Swanson. (CRKR.)

The Bavaria schoolhouse was established in District 17 in July 1869. Located in Bavaria, it was replaced with a brick building at a cost of $36,000 in 1925. The school offered competitive sports and produced many good basketball and baseball teams. After the school closed in 1956, the building became a warehouse for Augustine's Furniture Store. It now sits abandoned. (CRKR.)

Eight

SALINA, MARIPOSA, AND CHICO

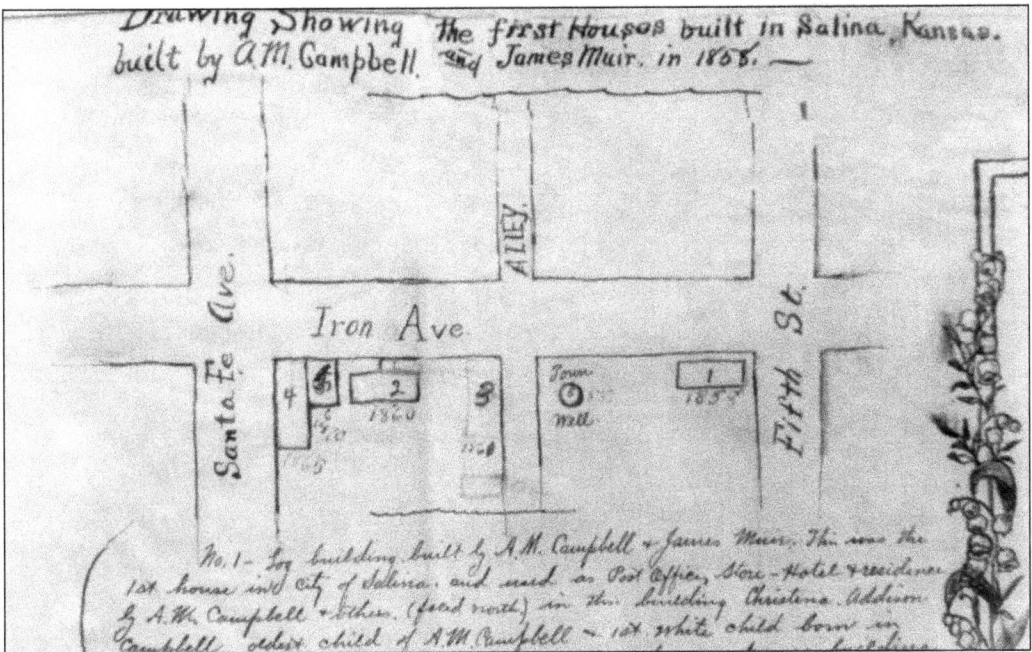

This drawing shows the first house that was built in Salina, Kansas, which was constructed by A.M. Campbell and James Muir in 1858. There was a well next to the house. Today, the land is in the downtown district and across from the community theater, where the new Burger King restaurant stands. (CRKR.)

Englishwoman Ms. Eglow visited Salina in 1905 and sent this photograph to her friend Edward as a token of herself to remind him of their love. According to the notes on the back of the photograph, she was too young at the time for proper courting, so they could not be seen with each other. (Authors' collection.)

The Iron Avenue Bridge in Salina is pictured in this postcard from the Missouri Valley Bridge and Iron Works on January 28, 1912. The bridge crosses the Smokey Hill River next to the cabin that A.M. Campbell and James Muir built. The building behind the bridge in the background is the H.D. Lee Mill. H.D. Lee was the designer of the original Lee Jeans. (Authors' collection.)

Iron Ave Bridge, Salina, Kansas

James R. Huiett stands in front of small wood-frame house on North Front Street in Salina. This photograph was taken on August 26, 1904. Settlers led by journalist and lawyer William A. Phillips founded Salina in 1858. Over the next two years, the territorial legislature chartered the town company, organized the surrounding area as Saline County, and named Salina the county seat. The westernmost town on the Smoky Hill Trail, Salina established itself as a trading post for westbound immigrants and prospectors bound for Pike's Peak. (Authors' collection.)

According to this www.princeton.edu document on Salina, Kansas, "This east-looking view shows Iron Avenue in Salina. There is a combination of horse-drawn carriages and early cars on the dirt road. The town expanded rapidly with the arrival of the Kansas Pacific Railway in 1867, and Salina was established as a city in 1870. The cattle trade arrived in 1872, transforming Salina into a cow town. During the 1870s, wheat became the dominant crop in the area and agriculture became the engine of the local economy. By 1880, the city was an area industrial center with several mills and a carriage and wagon factory." (Authors' collection.)

According to the www.kancoll.org website on Saline County, Laura Huiett stands in front of a small wood-frame house in Salina in August 1904. "While the town is located on both sides of the river, the greater part, including the entire business portion, is on the west side. It is somewhat in doubt as to who built the first house in town, but from the statements of the earliest settlers, there is no doubt that W.A. Phillips put up the first house ever erected in the city. It was a large log house and stood on what is now Iron Avenue, between Santa Fe Avenue and the river." (Authors' collection.)

Santa Fe Avenue in Salina is pictured here at the turn of the 20th century. Old cars mix with horse-drawn carriages on the road. The trolley is active, and the tracks can be seen running down Santa Fe Street. By 1930, Salina was ranked fifth in the world in flour production. Milling continued as a principal industry until the 1960s, when the Interstate Commerce Commission changed the rules on freight rates for flour as compared with rough grains. (Authors' collection.)

The cabin was built of hewn logs, with a clapboard roof, dirt floor, and ample stone fireplace. The structure was 18 by 26 feet. It was built around December 1856 by Coote Lombard and party and was mostly used for temporally shelter. The destruction of the cabin is unknown; a piece of the cabin is now at the Smoky Hill Museum. The cabin was originally located northeast of the city of Salina.

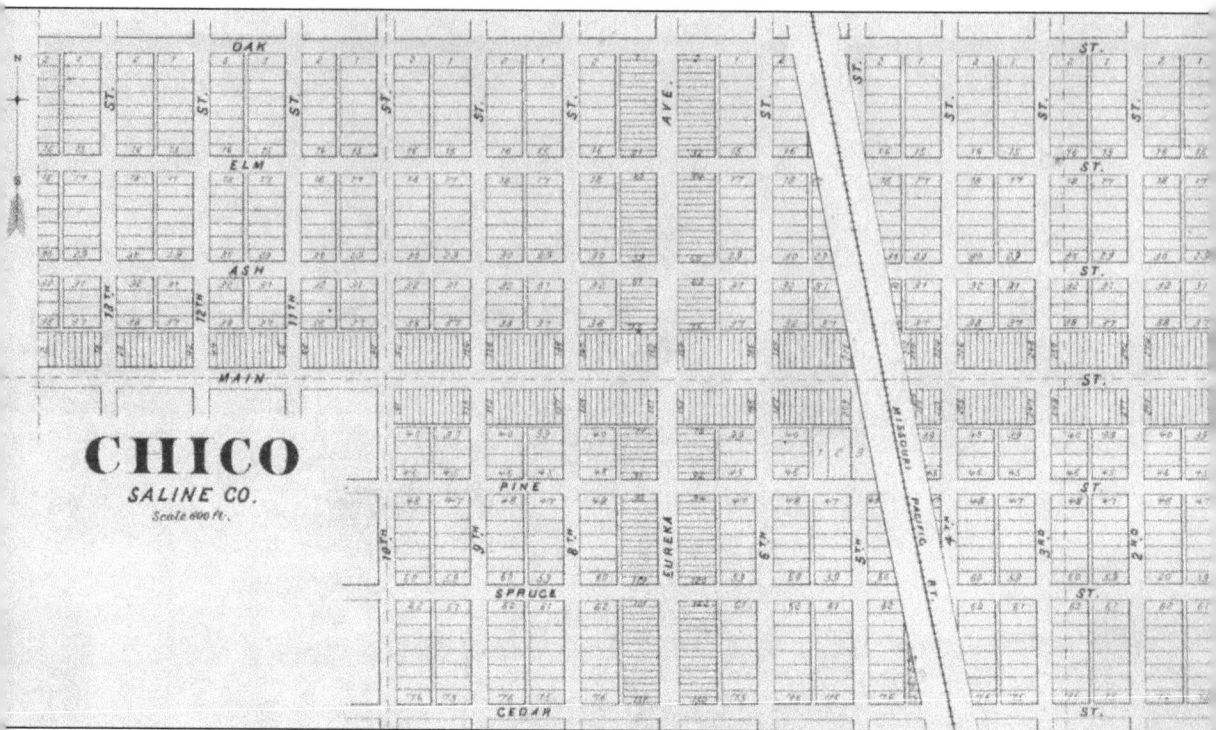

CHICO

SALINE CO.

Scale 600 ft.

Pictured here is an 1884 Edwards map of Chico, Kansas. On January 1, 1886, the town of Chico was platted by Chico Town Company, whose company officers were Anson Miller, Oscar Seitz, M.D. Teagne, and A.F. Harsh. The local newspaper was the *Chico Advertiser*. By February 1886, nearly 100 lots had been sold, and in a few months time, a depot, post office, grain elevator, drugstore, and livery stable were erected. Chico's demise began when the town of Gypsum was established in the same year. Chico's lumberyard was the first business to be moved to Gypsum after Chico lost its depot. The Missouri Pacific Railroad Company decided to move the depot to Kipp, Kansas. When it was moved early one Sunday morning, several railroad workers were arrested for violating the peace. Chico was gradually abandoned, and the town was vacated by the Kansas Legislature in 1895. (Authors' collection.)

Nine

SALINE COUNTY TODAY

A stone marker in Hallville, Kansas, is pictured in November 2010. The marker was built to honor the town of Hallville, which was active from 1888 to 1958. The town used to stand about five miles south of Saline on Simpson Road. It had a blacksmith shop, packhouse, railroad depot, elevator, chapel, and stockyard. The area was served by two schools and had a population of 13 people. In its heyday, the town was held together by Kristina Peterson, who acted as grain buyer, elevator operator, merchant, and housekeeper. When she passed away in 1958, the town died with her. Past residents remember Saturday get-togethers that included ice skating, hunting with ponies, dancing in the depot, bonfires, and storytelling. (Authors' collection.)

Bridgeport, Kansas, is pictured in 2010. Looking south on Main Street today, there is a concrete business, Zimmerman's Concrete, and ruins of the old bank remain in the area. The Bridgeport Flour Mill, built by Daniel T. Hopkins, is no longer a mill, and the cheese factory is gone as well. Nothing remains of the original town other than the history, and people are wary of living in the area because the town floods frequently. (Authors' collection.)

Cambria Mill's abandoned ruins are pictured in November 2010. The town of Glickville died in the early 1900s, and the mill was vacant in the 1920s. The ruins remain today as a reminder of the enterprising early history of Kansas. The Sanborn Cemetery was also forgotten for over 100 years. (Authors' collection.)

Glickville is now considered a Kansas ghost town. This November 2010 image shows the location of the long-lost community. After decades of abandonment, the town is no longer there; when the mill closed, the town did too. Businesses moved to New Cambria, and the townspeople relocated to other areas. (Authors' collection.)

This November 2011 photograph shows what remains of the abandoned Giersch house that is located on the Schippel farm. The Giersch family came to early Saline County in 1857, and they first settled on what is now the Schippel estate. The Giersch family was wealthy. The house was abandoned in the 1950s due to a massive fire. The property was maintained after Schippel passed away in 1906. (Authors' collection.)

In January 1982, the Gotthart Schippel house caught on fire and burned down. It had sat vacant for some years, and someone had started a fire in the house, perhaps to stay warm. Gotthart Schippel designed and built the house in the 1880s near the location of his famed ferry that crossed the river. When he passed away in 1906, Schippel was one of the largest landholders in the state. The house was then owned by his descendants, who no longer used it.

The sign is all that remains of the closed depot in Bavaria. Although trains still pass by and sometimes stop at the mill there, most of Bavaria's original buildings are gone, with the exception of the church and school, which are abandoned. (Authors' collection.)

This wood-frame church in Bavaria is no longer in service. The Lutheran Church was instrumental in the town's growth, providing spiritual support to those who settled in the area. Like many small towns, Bavaria's school and church relocated to a more central location. Wood-frame churches were often victim to fires and tornados, making them unsafe. (Authors' collection.)

Bavaria High School served as a factory warehouse after it closed. Now, the roof has decayed and trees have grown onto the school building. The students were relocated to a larger high school that serviced several small towns. (Authors' collection.)

This June 2013 photograph looks south down Main Street in Glendale, Kansas. Homes and buildings were moved to other locations, and many were torn down. The only buildings left are the old depot station and bank. The town declined over the years. (Authors' collection.)

Glendale State Bank is pictured in June 2013. Built in 1916, the Glendale State Bank closed when the Depression hit in 1932. Like the rest of the United States, the Depression was hard on the small communities of Kansas. The financial swings of wheat and cattle sales at this time were difficult on Glendale. (Authors' collection.)

This June 2013 photograph looks west on Second Street towards downtown Glendale. Although much of the growth of Saline County went to Salina, Glendale has managed to maintain some citizens. (Authors' collection.)

Pictured here is a view of Mentor, Kansas, looking east on Mentor Road in June 2013. Located a mile from Salina, the bedroom community of Mentor still has a fire station and a United Methodist church, as well as mail service through Salina. (Authors' collection.)

ABOUT THE AUTHORS

Dustin Ray Shannon, born and raised in Salina, Kansas, now interprets 1870s undertakers of Kansas at the Old Cow Town Museum in Wichita. He strives to preserve abandoned privately owned cemeteries and to serve as an advocate for the deceased in Kansas. He has previously worked on the Sanborn Cemetery Preservation and Restoration Project with Ada Wood. He is currently researching Kansas's extinct towns as he collects and preserves images and artifacts of Kansas. Formerly a volunteer at the Smoky Hill Museum in Salina, Dustin is the founder of the Shannon Historical Research group, which can be found online at crownpoint.weebly.com.

Faith Dincolo, MFA, is a filmmaker and writer who researches and writes about Kansas history and genealogy. Her family settled parts of Kansas and has cemeteries on the Chisholm Trail in southern Kansas.

Visit us at
arcadiapublishing.com

www.ingramcontent.com/pod-product-compliance
Lightning Source LLC
Chambersburg PA
CBHW050548110426
42813CB00008B/2296